student WORKBOOK

AQA A2 Health & Social Care

Richard Smithson

Philip Allan Updates, Market Place, Deddington,
Oxfordshire, OX15 0SE

Orders

Bookpoint Ltd, 130 Milton Park, Abingdon,
Oxfordshire, OX14 4SB
tel: 01235 827720   fax: 01235 400454
e-mail: uk.orders@bookpoint.co.uk

Lines are open 9.00 a.m.–5.00 p.m., Monday to Saturday, with
a 24-hour message answering service. You can also order
through the Philip Allan Updates website: www.philipallan.co.uk

© Richard Smithson

ISBN-13: 978-1-84489-468-0   ISBN-10: 1-84489-468-1

Printed in Spain

Environmental information
The paper on which this title is printed is sourced
from managed, sustainable forests.

P00741

Introduction

This workbook covers material relating to the compulsory and optional A2 units of the AQA GCE Health and Social Care specifications. It can be used in conjunction with the textbook *AQA A2 Health & Social Care* published by Philip Allan Updates.

Section 1 contains exercises for Unit 12: Human Development: Factors and Theories.

Section 2 contains exercises for Unit 13: The Role of Exercise in Maintaining Health and Well-being.

Section 3 contains exercises for Unit 14: Diagnosis and Treatment.

Section 4 contains exercises for Unit 15: Clients with Disabilities.

Section 5 contains guidance and exercises on answering data-response questions.

Section 1 Human development: factors and theories

Topic 1 Theories of development

Exercise 1 Piaget's theory of cognitive development

Key concepts

1 Peter can knit. He is not knitting at the moment, but he has a set of mental structures that enable him to produce knitting behaviour at any time. What are these mental structures called?

2 Irma enjoys stacking wooden cubes to build a tower. Her aunt gives her a set of plastic beakers of different sizes, so that each beaker just fits inside the next larger beaker.

Irma tries to stack the beakers up. However, she finds that a larger beaker will not stack on top of a smaller one, so she soon learns to start with the largest beaker at the bottom and to put successively smaller beakers on top.

a State what is meant by assimilation.

b From the description above, identify an example of assimilation.

c State what is meant by accommodation.

d From the description above, identify an example of accommodation.

e Toys are sometimes designed to help infants to develop particular concepts. For example, different coloured objects can help to develop colour concept. Name **one** concept that the stacking beakers described above might help to develop.

f Notice that Irma does not have to be taught concepts, or be told what to do with the beakers. She learns by playing. Name this type of learning.

Stages of development

3 Decide which of Piaget's stages of cognitive development each of the following children has reached.

 a Juanita is shopping with her father, brother and sister. At one point, Juanita tells her father that he should not buy a tin of beans that is dented. He asks why not and she replies that it will contain fewer beans than an undented tin.

 b Juanita's sister points out that the dent cannot have made any difference to the number of beans in the tin.

 c Juanita's brother suggests that if a food company made dents in all its tins, people might buy them because they were different from everyone else's.

4 a Name the cognitive ability that Juanita's sister showed in **3b**, but that Juanita did not show.

 b According to Piaget's stage theory, what might vary between different children as they progress through the stages?

 c According to Piaget's stage theory, what will be the same in all children as they progress through the stages?

5 a What does the word 'sensorimotor' indicate about a child's awareness in the early sensorimotor stage?

 b Define 'object permanence'.

 c Suggest a simple way of making an object 'disappear' in an object permanence test.

d How did Bower and Wishart make an object disappear in their study of object permanence?

....

e Draw **one** conclusion from Bower and Wishart's study.

....

6 a In the preoperational stage, what is it that the child cannot yet perform?

....

b According to Piaget, what is egocentrism?

....

c Piaget used ten cards in the mountains test. What did the cards depict?

....

d A child who is no longer egocentric is able to…

....

e Why did Hughes use walls, a policeman doll and a boy doll instead of mountains in his test of egocentrism?

....

f A child in the intuitive period of the preoperational stage tends to judge by…

....

7 One conservation test is based on the conservation of number. This can be performed using buttons.
a What is conserved in this conservation test?

....

b What is varied in this conservation test?

....

c In a conservation of number test, a student asks a child, 'Now, are there more buttons in one row?' What is wrong with this question?

....

d Write a correct version of the question in part **c**.

e Apart from conservation of number, suggest **two** other quantities that could feature in conservation tests.

f Why did McGarrigle and Donaldson use a 'naughty teddy' in their test of conservation?

g Mental operations performed using real objects or objects that can be visualised are called **concrete** operations. What are mental operations performed on abstract concepts called?

h 'What would it be like if…' is an example of a particular type of question. Which type?

Exercise 2 Skinner's learning theory

1 What, according to behaviourists, is the subject matter of psychology?

2 Learning theory is really a theory about how individuals acquire…

3 According to learning theory, what consequence of an action is likely to reinforce that action?

4 What is the behaviour that is reinforced in a simple Skinner box designed for a pigeon?

5 Name the technique of rewarding successively closer approximations to the required behaviour.

6 Name the important type of psychological process that was ignored by behaviourists.

Exercise 3 Social learning theory

A Social learning theory emphasises three key processes in learning:
  a reinforcement
  b modelling
  c the extraction of cognitions

Decide which of these processes is best illustrated by each of the following examples. Write the appropriate letter in each box.

1 After watching a rap video, William starts wearing his baseball cap sideways.

2 Teresa's accent changes after spending her first term at university.

3 The first time Deanne asked a question in class, the teacher praised her, so she often asks questions now.

4 After his first few days at work, Jaroslaw realised that it was not acceptable to make jokes about people of other races.

5 Ben's older sister asked him what he had learned at school that day. He replied, 'Not to swear when the teachers can hear'.

B1 Suggest **three** different agents of socialisation that might be present in a child's home.

2 Suggest **one** agent of socialisation that never rewards or punishes a child's behaviour.

3 The children in the experimental and control groups in Bandura's 1965 experiment were treated in slightly different ways. Give **two** things that the children in the control group were asked to do.

4 Give **one** reason for having a control group in an experiment.

....

Exercise 4 Freud's theory of psychosexual development

1 Name the part of the personality sometimes described as:
   a the reality principle

....

   b the moral part of the self

....

   c the pleasure principle

....

2 Name **three** kinds of instinctual energy that are supposed to motivate behaviour.

....

....

3 State **one** other important idea that Freud had about human motivation.

....

4 A newborn baby boy is hardly aware of what is going on around him. He does not have any moral beliefs. He demands immediate gratification of his needs by crying when he feels hunger or discomfort.
   a Link each of the above statements with Freud's three parts of the personality.

Personality part	Statement

   b In which stage of psychosexual development is this baby likely to be?

....

5 Which **two** parts of the personality are in conflict when a person is tempted to do something he or she believes to be wrong?

6 According to Freud, during which stage of psychosexual development does the ego develop?

7 According to Freud, what (possibly hidden) feelings will a child in the phallic stage have towards:
a the same-sex parent

b the opposite-sex parent

8 a Name the conflict boys are assumed to experience during the phallic stage.

b According to Freud, what process resolves the conflicts experienced during the phallic stage?

c Which part of the personality develops as a result of this process?

Exercise 5 Bowlby's theory of attachment

Theory and practice

1 Name the period of a child's life during which Bowlby believed that attachment must occur, if it is to be successful.

2 Bowlby believed that a single strong attachment was superior to multiple attachments. Name this idea.

3 Give **one** reason why multiple attachments might actually be better for a child than a single attachment.

4 According to Bowlby, if a child is separated from his or her own parents, is it better for the child to be adopted or reared in a large institution?

5 Give **one** alternative parent-substitute arrangement, apart from those mentioned above.

6 List **three** short-term effects of separation that were described by Bowlby.

7 List **four** long-term harmful effects that Bowlby believed could result from maternal deprivation.

8 Name the **two** different sorts of disturbance of attachment that Rutter described, as a replacement for Bowlby's term 'maternal deprivation'.

9 Give **three** different formal day-care arrangements for young children.

Key studies

10 Tizard's studies of children in care found that most of the children who were adopted developed more satisfactory relationships with their adoptive parents than children returned to their natural parents.
a Give **one** likely reason for this difference.

b Do Tizard's studies support Bowlby's view that family rearing of children is superior to care in a residential home?

c Do Tizard's studies support Bowlby's view that there is a critical period in the development of attachment?

d What sort of participants did Tizard use as her control group?

11 a Give **two** factors that, according to Rutter's 1981 study, were likely to lead to harmful effects when associated with separation.

b Give **two** circumstances leading to separation that, according to Rutter's 1981 study, were less likely to lead to harmful effects.

12 a During the first 3 minutes of each trial, who is present in the room in Ainsworth's 'strange situation'?

b What behaviour would be expected of a securely attached child during the first 3 minutes in the strange situation?

c Suggest **two** behaviours that would be expected of a securely attached child when the mother leaves the room during the strange situation.

d In Ainsworth's strange situation, who is present in the room immediately after the mother leaves it?

e Name the **two** types of insecure attachment described by Ainsworth.

f Ainsworth assumed that the type of attachment shown by infants depends on the parenting behaviour they have experienced. Name this assumption.

13 Give **one** alternative explanation of a link between a parent's behaviour and the behaviour of a child.

Topic 2 Areas of development

Exercise 1 Attachment

A The development of attachment has been divided into four stages (**a–d**):
   a the indiscriminate attachment stage
   b the stage of multiple attachments
   c the asocial stage
   d the stage of specific attachments

Decide the order in which these stages occur, starting with the earliest. Write your answers in the boxes.

  1 ▆
  2 ▆
  3 ▆
  4 ▆

B1 List **three** proximity-maintaining behaviours shown by attached infants.

  2 A child is likely to be least able to tolerate separation from familiar adults at which of the following ages:
   a 4 months
   b 14 months
   c 4 years

C1 Name **two** theories of development that suggest that attachment results from the pleasure of feeding.

  2 A cognitive explanation for attachment suggests that it will develop once a particular cognitive ability has been achieved. Name that ability.

3 Outline an ethological explanation for:

a attachment

b the timing of the onset of attachment

Exercise 2 Prosocial and antisocial behaviour

1 Suggest **two** prosocial behaviours that might be produced by children in a nursery school setting.

2 Give **two** specific antisocial behaviours that are relatively common among young children.

3 Give **one** biological explanation for differences in levels or frequency of aggression between different individuals of the same sex.

4 Give **two** social learning explanations that might be used to explain why the children of aggressive parents are more likely to be aggressive than the children of non-aggressive parents.

5 Name the researcher who, in 1965, studied aggression in children, using the experimental method.

6 Does the study referred to in Question **5** tend to support or refute a learning-theory explanation for aggression? Justify your answer.

7 Outline why, according to Freud, a 6-year-old child is likely to produce more prosocial and less anti-social behaviour than a 3-year-old child.

Exercise 3 Sex differences in behaviour and abilities

One type of behaviour in which there is a significant difference between men and women is in occupational choices.

1 a Suggest **one** other type of behaviour in which there is a significant difference between men and women.

b Give **one** possible biological explanation for this difference.

2 a Suggest **two** small (but genuine) differences in abilities between the sexes.

b Give **one** reason to suggest why these differences might be influenced by maturation.

3 When she was a little girl, Rachel was often rewarded for showing an interest in hair styling. Now she wants to be a hairdresser.

Name **two** theories of development that suggest that behaviour can be influenced by rewards.

4 Name **one** other theory that suggests that sex differences can occur because children identify with the parent who is the same sex as themselves.

Exercise 4 Language development

1 List **three** stages in language development, in the order in which they occur.

2 Skinner's learning theory suggests that language is acquired only if language behaviour is...

....

3 Name the psychologist who suggested that all children are born with a language-acquisition device.

....

4 a Name the non-existent animal that Berko used in his 1958 study of children's use of grammatical rules.

....

b Which particular rule was this animal used to test?

....

5 Children's learning of grammatical rules can be explained by which feature of social learning theory?

....

....

Exercise 5 Parenting styles

1 Name the parental style illustrated by each of the following examples:
 a George's children often fight with each other. George usually ignores their behaviour, unless it interferes with what he is doing, in which case he gets very angry suddenly and punishes them harshly.

....

 b Tamsin's house is very clean and neat. She does not allow her children to make a noise or run about in the house, in case they damage anything. Occasionally she kisses them, but she will not let them cuddle her in case her clothes get creased.

....

 c When Jiri's children are naughty, he usually explains why he does not approve of their behaviour. On Friday evenings, they all sit down together to plan what they will do at the weekend.

....

2 Explain why studies such as those by Sears, Maccoby and Levin, and Baumrind, do not prove that parental styles influence the behaviour of children.

3 Name **one** non-environmental factor that might explain why some children are more aggressive than others.

Topic 3 Factors affecting development

Exercise 1 Nature and nurture

1 Complete the table by stating whether each of the factors that can influence development is a nature factor or a nurture factor.

Factor	Nature/nurture
a Parenting style	
b Nutrition	
c Genotype	
d Exercise	
e Maturation	

2 There are several features of development that are influenced by genetics. These include universality and development in an invariant sequence.
   a Outline what is meant by saying that a type of development is universal.

   b Name **one** theory that suggests an invariant sequence of development.

   c Give **two** *other* features of genetically influenced behaviour (apart from universality and development in an invariant sequence).

d Give **one** reason why the rooting reflex is likely to be genetically determined.

e Suggest **two** areas of development that might be most likely to occur during a critical period.

f Give **two** biological environmental factors that can influence development.

g Define maturation.

3 a What is the name given to the molecule that forms chromosomes.

b Name **one** type of human cell that contains 23 chromosomes.

c What is the name given to an individual's complete set of genetic material?

d What are sections of a chromosome that determine an individual's physical and psychological characteristics called?

e Under what circumstance can two individuals have exactly the same genetic material?

f How many chromosomes directly determine the sex of an individual?

Section 2 The role of exercise in maintaining health and well-being

Topic 1 Exercise-related fitness

Exercise 1 Fitness definitions

Here are seven terms related to different kinds of fitness (**a–g**) and their definitions.

Match the terms with their definitions, writing your answers in the boxes. The first definition has been done for you.

a mobility
b muscular fitness
c stamina
d aerobic fitness
e dynamic strength
f maximum strength
g flexibility

1 The capacity of a person's muscles to exert force   **b**
2 The ability to continue to exert strength over an extended period without excessive fatigue ☐
3 A person's capacity to take up and use sufficient oxygen to sustain work over a long period ☐
4 The range of movement without pain that people have in their mobile joints ☐
5 The power of a muscle to contract at speed, while overcoming resistance ☐
6 The greatest force a muscle can exert in a single contraction ☐
7 The ability to move with speed, balance, and/or endurance ☐

Exercise 2 Fitness examples

After many years of running on roads, Howard can run at 10 kph for 20 minutes without feeling tired. He can run for 30 kilometres without stopping to rest. He finds it difficult and painful to step up onto a chair.

State whether, in Howard's case, each of the following is good or poor. In each case back up your comments with reference to the description of Howard.

1 Howard's stamina

....

2 Howard's flexibility

....

3 Howard's aerobic fitness

....

Exercise 3 The physiology of aerobic fitness

Aerobic fitness requires effective external respiration, oxygen transport and oxygen uptake within cells.

1 What is external respiration?

2 a Oxygen is transported around the body attached to molecules of which chemical compound?

   b What transports these molecules, combined with oxygen, around the body?

3 Name the gas that is a by-product of cellular respiration.

4 a In which organs are the alveoli?

   b State **two** important processes that take place in the alveoli.

5 Name **two** nutrient chemicals that are used in cellular respiration to do work.

6 a Name the process by which nutrients are converted into pyruvate.

   b Name the process in which pyruvate is oxidised.

7 Name the chemical, produced by anaerobic respiration, that builds up in the muscles, causing them to ache during and immediately after strenuous exercise.

Exercise 4 Short-term physiological effects of training

1 Give **two** short-term effects of exercise on the action of the heart.

2 Give **one** short-term effect of exercise on capillaries that serve muscles.

3 State the short-term effect of exercise on blood pressure.

4 Give **two** short-term effects of exercise on ventilation.

5 Give **two** short-term effects of exercise on the skin.

Exercise 5 Long-term physiological effects of training

1 State **one** long-term effect of exercise on blood pressure.

2 State the long-term effect of exercise on resting pulse rate.

3 State **two** long-term effects of exercise on blood vessels.

4 Apart from the effects on the respiratory and cardiovascular systems, give **two** other long-term effects of exercise on body tissues.

Topic 2 Measuring and monitoring fitness

Exercise 1 VO$_2$max

1 State how VO$_2$max is calculated. Remember to include the units of measurement.

....

....

2 Colin has a body weight of 100 kilograms. When exercising at maximum effort, Colin uses 6 litres of oxygen every minute. Calculate Colin's VO$_2$max.

....

3 Danuta's VO$_2$max is half that of Colin's, but so is her body weight. Calculate how many litres of oxygen Danuta will use at maximum effort.

....

4 Naomi has a VO$_2$max of 40 millilitres per kilogram per minute. She uses 2400 millilitres of oxygen per minute at maximum effort. What is her body weight?

....

Exercise 2 Body mass index (BMI)

A State how BMI is calculated. Remember to include units of measurement.

....

....

B For each of the BMIs, choose the appropriate letter (**a–d**) from the list below. Write your answers in the boxes.

a underweight
b within the range of normal
c overweight
d obese

1 Clare has a BMI of 27.
2 Yukiko has a BMI of 17.
3 Aled has a BMI of 31.
4 Kapil has a BMI of 20.

C Calculate the BMIs of the following individuals. Give your answers to 1 decimal place.

1 Paolo is 1.90 m tall and weighs 65 kg.

2 Jo is 1.54 m tall and weighs 51 kg.

3 Irina is 1.80 m tall and weighs 94 kg.

D People with a BMI of 29 might be classified as 'overweight'. In most cases this will mean that they have excessive amounts of body fat. Under what circumstances might a person have a BMI of 29 without having excessive body fat?

Exercise 3 Pulse rate

1 Resting pulse rate is higher than normal in people who are unwell and/or unfit and people who are very old. Give **one** other group whose members have high resting pulse rates.

2 For each of the following adults, state whether the resting pulse rate is below average, within the average range or above average.

a Clare has a resting pulse rate of 76 bpm.

b Yukiko has a resting pulse rate of 65 bpm.

c Aled has a resting pulse rate of 85 bpm.

d Kapil has a resting pulse rate of 50 bpm.

3 Judging only on the basis of their resting pulse rates:
  a Name the fittest of the adults listed in Question **2**.

  b Name the least fit of the adults listed in Question **2**.

Exercise 4 Lung function tests

A1 State what is meant by peak expiratory flow rate (peak flow).

2 a A peak-flow meter can be used to measure lung function. Name a different instrument that can also be used to measure peak flow.

  b Give **two** advantages of the peak-flow meter compared with the alternative instrument.

  c Give **one** disadvantage of the peak-flow meter compared with the alternative instrument.

B For each of the following adults, state whether the peak flow is below average, within the average range or above average.

  1 Clare has a peak flow of 315 l/min.

  2 Yukiko has a peak flow of 420 l/min.

  3 Aled has a peak flow of 550 l/min.

  4 Kapil has a peak flow of 680 l/min.

C Suggest **one** medical condition that might explain Clare's peak-flow rate.

....

D Here are six terms related to different measures of lung function (**a–f**) and their definitions.

Match the terms with their definitions, writing your answers in the boxes.

a minute ventilation
b tidal volume
c peak expiratory flow rate

d resting breathing rate
e forced vital capacity
f VO$_2$max

1 The total volume of air breathed out of the lungs on a forced expiration following full inspiration

2 The maximum rate of flow in litres per minute out of the lungs on a forced expiration

3 Tidal volume multiplied by breathing rate

4 The maximum volume of oxygen a person can use per minute per kilogram of body mass

5 The number of breaths taken per minute while at rest

6 The volume of air inspired and expired during a normal breath

Exercise 5 Perceived exertion scales

1 Don and Julie both run on a treadmill at 8 mph for 5 minutes. Near the end of the exercise, Don rates his exertion at 20 and Julie rates her exertion at 15. Which person is probably fitter? Justify your answer.

....

2 Suggest **one** measure that could be used to find out how long it took Don and Julie to recover from their exertion.

....

3 Give **two** reasons why VO$_2$max is a better measure of aerobic fitness than perceived exertion.

....

Exercise 6 Benefits of exercise

Exercise and disease prevention

1 Suggest **one** way in which exercise can help to prevent or reduce the risk of both diabetes and obesity.

....

2 List **two** other diseases that can be prevented by taking regular exercise.

3 List **two** other diseases that can be reduced by taking regular exercise.

Weight control

4 Suggest **two** ways in which exercise helps people avoid becoming overweight.

5 Name the brain mechanism that is believed to control appetite.

Psychological benefits

6 Name **two** types of chemical that are released in the brain during exercise and which contribute to a feeling of well-being.

7 Give **three** likely psychological benefits of exercise.

Topic 3 Risks and precautions

Exercise 1 Risks

1 a Suggest **one** type of injury that is likely to occur in both football and skiing.

b Give **two** sports in which protection from head injuries is necessary.

c Suggest **one** chronic condition that can result from an earlier joint injury.

2 Aziz, Bernard and Colin are all aged 40. They are the same weight and height and are heavier than the average male of their age. Aziz never takes any exercise. At the moment, he is watching television. Bernard has never taken any exercise until today. At the moment, he is struggling to keep up on a treadmill at the gym. Colin exercises regularly at the gym and specialises in weight training. At the moment, he is relaxing in a bath.

Use the information above to answer the following questions.
a Which of the three men is most likely to have the lowest pulse rate?

b Which of the three men is most likely to suffer a stroke or heart attack?

c Which of the three men is most likely to have the highest maximum blood pressure?

d Suggest why Colin is the same weight as the other men, even though he takes more exercise. In your answer, refer to two types of body tissue.

3 Apart from exercise, give **four** factors that influence a person's aerobic fitness.

Exercise 2 Precautions

1 a Suggest **one** practitioner who might carry out a medical check on an unfit person before s/he starts an exercise programme.

b Suggest **one** test this practitioner might carry out to determine whether the person might be at risk of a stroke.

2 Suggest **one** practitioner who can give expert advice on exercise to a person who is recovering from injury.

....

3 Give **three** functions of clothing that is designed for use in sports and exercise.

....

....

....

4 Suggest **two** ways in which warming up before exercise reduces risks.

....

....

5 Give **two** undesirable effects of exercise that can be reduced by warming down.

....

Topic 4 Barriers to exercise

Exercise 1 Examples of barriers

1 Emma works part-time at a checkout in a town-centre supermarket. She has very little money to spare after paying for rent and food. Although she has never taken exercise before, she now feels that she ought to join a gym to try to lose some weight.

From the description above, identify **two** likely barriers that might make it difficult for Emma to exercise. Link each barrier with a piece of information given in the description.

Barrier: .... Link: ....

Barrier: .... Link: ....

2 Suggest **two** barriers to participation that might affect a wealthy single parent living in Cornwall with young children and whose chosen sport is skiing. Link each barrier with a piece of information given in the description.

Barrier: .... Link: ....

Barrier: .... Link: ....

Topic 5 Exercise programmes

Exercise 1 Needs of clients

1 Suggest **three** different groups of clients who could benefit from exercise programmes. In each case, suggest what the purpose of a programme might be.

....

....

....

2 Apart from the five principles of good practice and safety, suggest **three** features or principles that should be included in an exercise programme designed for a particular client.

....

....

....

Section 3 Diagnosis and treatment

Topic 1 Diagnosis

Exercise 1 GP consultation

1 a During a consultation, a GP interviews the patient to find out what is wrong and also to find important background information. What is this process called?

b List **three** kinds of background information a GP might seek, in addition to enquiring about symptoms.

2 What is the difference between the signs and the symptoms of disease?

3 Each of the techniques described below might feature in a physical examination. Name each technique.
   a The GP uses a rubber hammer to tap the patient's knee, just below the patella.

   b The GP looks into the patient's ears.

   c The GP feels the patient's abdomen.

4 Measurements of blood pressure yield two figures, for example 120/80.
   a Name the type of blood pressure that produces the first figure.

   b Name the type of blood pressure that produces the second figure.

   c In what units is blood pressure measured?

d Name the piece of equipment that is used to measure blood pressure.

5 a Name **two** body fluids that are commonly collected by GPs and sent for analysis in diagnostic tests.

b Suggest **two** ways in which computers can aid diagnosis.

Exercise 2 Survey techniques

1 Name **two** survey methods.

2 Give **two** advantages of asking closed questions.

3 a A question that allows a respondent an unlimited opportunity to respond is called an…

b Give **one** advantage of this type of question.

Topic 2 Diagnostic techniques

Exercise 1 Imaging techniques

Ultrasound

1 a Apart from the fact that it is inaudible, how does ultrasound differ from sound that people can hear?

b Give **one** common use of ultrasound scanning.

....

c Name **one** sort of tissue that cannot be penetrated by ultrasound.

....

X-rays
2 a What sort of radiation is used in X-ray scanning?

....

b Why do bones appear dark on an X-ray image?

....

c Name the technique that uses X-rays to detect abnormalities in women's breasts.

....

d Suggest **two** disadvantages of the use of X-rays as an imaging technique.

....

....

e Name the contrast medium that is used in contrast X-rays.

....

f Name the body system that is most likely to be scanned using contrast X-rays.

....

CT scanning
3 a In CT scanning, what do the letters CT stand for?

....

b Give **one** advantage of CT scanning compared with a standard X-ray.

....

c Give **one** disadvantage of CT scanning compared with a standard X-ray.

....

MRI scanning

4 a In MRI scanning, what do the letters MRI stand for?

b What sort of radiation is used in MRI scanning?

c Give **one** advantage of MRI scanning compared with both standard X-rays and CT scanning.

d Name **one** organ that can be imaged effectively using MRI scanning and which cannot be scanned using standard or contrast X-rays.

PET scanning

5 a In PET scanning, what do the letters PET stand for?

b What type of substance has to be introduced into the body before PET scanning can begin?

c Give **one** disadvantage of PET scanning, which is not shared by MRI scanning.

6 Give **one** advantage of all the methods of scanning mentioned in Questions **1–5**, compared with an endoscopic examination.

Exercise 2 Other diagnostic techniques

1 Name the technique in which a small piece of tissue is taken from the body for cytological examination.

2 Name the technique in which a camera is inserted into a body cavity for observation purposes.

3 Name the technique that measures the electrical activity of the circulatory system.

....

4 a Chorionic villus sampling is an example of which type of technique?

....

  b Name the scanning technique that is used to assist in chorionic villus sampling.

....

5 Apart from blood and urine, name **one** body fluid, present in all people, that can be tested for the presence of organisms that cause infectious disease.

....

6 Apart from the body fluids mentioned above, name a fluid that is sometimes sampled in antenatal testing.

....

Topic 3 Treatment

Exercise 1 Drug treatments

1 A patient is prescribed three drugs. One is a diuretic, one is an anti-depressant and one is an opioid.
  a Which of the three drugs listed above is an example of a drug classified by chemical make-up?

....

  b Which of the three is an example of a drug classified by its effect on the body?

....

  c Which of the three is an example of a drug classified by the disorder treated?

....

2 a Suggest **one** form in which a drug can be used as a topical treatment.

....

b Give **two** reasons why some drugs must be administered by injection.

c Give **two** advantages of administering drugs by mouth.

d Suggest **one** slow-release form of a drug that avoids the drug being destroyed by the digestive system.

e Give **one** justification for prescribing drugs with harmful adverse side-effects.

Exercise 2 Surgery

A1 Give **one** example of surgery to implant a mechanical device.

2 Give **one** example of the use of reconstructive surgery.

3 Give **one** example of surgery in which tissue is removed.

B1 Suggest **three** precautions that are used to create aseptic conditions during surgery.

2 Apart from the risk of infection, give **two** risks that are associated with major surgery.

3 Give **two** advantages of the use of local rather than general anaesthesia.

C Here are five types of surgery (**a–e**) and their definitions. Match each type of surgery with its correct definition. Write your answers in the boxes.

a microsurgery
b transplant surgery
c major surgery
d endoscopic surgery
e laser surgery

1 Surgery in which tissue or organs are transferred from one person's body to another person's body
2 Surgery in which cutting is done by intense light rather than a metal tool
3 Surgery involving opening the cranium, chest or abdomen
4 Surgery requiring the use of miniature surgical tools
5 Procedures commonly known as 'keyhole surgery'

Exercise 3 Other treatments

1 a Explain how external radiotherapy is applied so as to target diseased tissue while doing minimal damage to the other tissues through which the radiation passes.

b Give **one** other way in which radiotherapy can be applied to a precise point within a person's body.

c Give **two** short-term adverse effects of exposure to ionising radiation.

2 a Dialysis is necessary because of the failure of which organs?

b Name the dialysis technique that removes waste products from the patient's blood outside the patient's body.

c Name the dialysis technique that is used for non-emergency dialysis.

3 a Name the technique used to break up gallstones and kidney stones, without the need for surgery.

b What sort of radiation is used to break up the stones?

Exercise 4 Factors affecting treatment

1 Suggest **two** factors an elderly patient might consider when deciding whether to go ahead with a treatment for cancer or to refuse treatment.

2 Suggest **one** lifestyle factor that is likely to reduce the effectiveness of treatment for a respiratory disease.

3 Suggest **one** lifestyle factor that is likely to increase the effectiveness of treatment for heart disease.

4 Suggest **three** other factors (apart from those related directly to lifestyle) that can influence the effectiveness of medical treatments.

Section 4 Clients with disabilities

Topic 1 Definitions and causes of disability

Exercise 1 Definitions

1 Name the model of disability that suggests that disability is the result not only of impairment but also the way society treats people with impairments.

2 What is the general name for a type of disability that leads to loss of movement, for example loss of mobility.

3 What is the general name for a disability such as blindness, deafness or loss of skin sensation.

4 Name a third type of disability, other than those you named in your answers to questions **2** and **3**.

Exercise 2 Causes

A Impairments result from a number of causes, including:
   a lifestyle-related diseases
   b chromosomal abnormalities
   c age-related disease conditions
   d genetic factors
   e nutritional effects on fetuses

For each of the conditions listed below, give one of the above causes (use each cause once only). Write an appropriate letter in each box.
   1 Spina bifida
   2 Osteoporosis
   3 Cystic fibrosis
   4 Down's syndrome
   5 Chronic obstructive pulmonary disease

B1 Suggest **three** causes of brain damage.

....

2 Name **one** disability condition that is more likely in people who are elderly, overweight and who have a genetic predisposition to the condition.

....

Exercise 3 The nervous system

1 Name **two** components of the central nervous system.

....

2 What basic function do all neurons have?

....

3 Name the substance that gives nerve tissue its white appearance.

....

4 a Sensory neurons transmit information from where to where?

....

b Motor neurons transmit information from where to where?

....

5 How are nerve impulses transmitted from one neuron to another?

....

6

A ....

B ....

C ....

D ....

Name the parts labelled **A**, **B**, **C** and **D** on the diagram of the left cerebral hemisphere of the brain.

Exercise 4 Localisation of function

1 Following a head injury, Satvinder has lost all feeling in his left arm. In which area of which lobe of which hemisphere has the damage occurred?

2 What is meant by paralysis?

3 Damage to which areas of the cerebral cortex leads to paralysis?

4 Following a stroke, Bruno can still understand what is said to him, but his speech is very hesitant and garbled. Which area of the cortex, in which hemisphere, is most likely to have been damaged by the stroke?

Topic 2 Disability conditions

Exercise 1 Cystic fibrosis

1 Cystic fibrosis is caused by a type of gene that only gives rise to the condition if a person has two copies of the gene. What is this type of gene called?

2 What is the name for a person who has just one copy of the cystic fibrosis gene?

3 A man and a woman each have one copy of the cystic fibrosis gene. They are planning to have a child together. What is the probability that any one of their children will have the disease?

4 Which of the following signs or symptoms commonly occur in cases of cystic fibrosis? Tick any that apply.
   a learning disability
   b a salty skin
   c sticky mucus in the lungs
   d being overweight

5 What physiotherapy treatment is usually required daily by children with cystic fibrosis?

6 Why do people with cystic fibrosis need special diets?

Exercise 2 Duchenne muscular dystrophy (DMD)

1 a What percentage of boys who have one recessive gene for DMD will have the disease?

   b What percentage of girls who have one recessive gene for DMD will have the disease?

2 DMD leads to muscle weakness. Give **three** noticeable effects of this weakness on a child's behaviour.

3 Give **two** reasons why children with DMD are less likely to do well at school than able-bodied children.

4 Name **one** technique that a physiotherapist can use to maintain flexibility in a child with DMD, without tiring the child.

Exercise 3 Down's syndrome

1 How many chromosomes does a person with Down's syndrome have in any one typical body cell?

2 What is the main disabling effect of Down's syndrome?

3 What is the main factor that increases the probability of having a baby with Down's syndrome?

4 Name **two** tests that can be used to detect Down's syndrome early in pregnancy.

Exercise 4 Cerebral palsy

1 All causes of cerebral palsy involve damage to which organ?

2 Give **two** ways in which the damage that leads to cerebral palsy could be caused.

3 Give **two** communication skills that are often impaired in cases of cerebral palsy.

4 Give **one** effect of cerebral palsy on motor development in infants.

Exercise 5 Spina bifida

1 Give **two** risks that result from nerve tissue being exposed in a severe case of spina bifida.

2 Give **one** technique by which a visual image of a fetus can be obtained to check for spina bifida.

3 Give **two** risk factors for spina bifida.

4 Give **two** impairments that could result from severe damage to the spinal cord.

Exercise 6 Multiple sclerosis (MS)

1 In MS, nerve transmission is affected by the loss of which substance from the nerve fibres?

2 Where are the plaques of scar tissue found in cases of MS?

3 Give **two** sensory symptoms of MS.

4 Give **two** motor signs of MS.

5 What is the name given to a symptomless period experienced by some people with MS?

Exercise 7 Alzheimer's disease

Alzheimer's disease can lead to the following:
   a lack of inhibition
   b aphasia
   c disorientation
   d action slips
   e confusion

Match each of the above terms to one of the following descriptions. Write the appropriate letter in each box.
   1 An elderly woman mistakes her son for her husband (who is dead).
   2 A person cannot remember the names of ordinary objects, such as chairs, and instead says, 'The thing you sit on'.
   3 A man in the dayroom of a residential home takes all his clothes off because he is too hot.
   4 A woman loses her way on the familiar journey to the shops.
   5 A man loses his glasses and later finds them in the fridge.

Exercise 8 Osteoarthritis

1 Give **one** visible sign of osteoarthitis in finger joints.

2 Name **one** audible sign that sometimes occurs in cases of osteoarthritis.

3 Give a reason why osteoarthritis can reduce mobility.

4 Suggest a treatment a GP might prescribe for osteoarthritis.

5 Suggest a surgical procedure that might help to improve mobility in a person with osteoarthritis.

6 Name **one** type of practitioner who can give advice and suggestions to help a person with osetoarthritis to maintain flexibility.

7 Name **one** type of practitioner who can give advice on suitable aids and adaptations.

Exercise 9 Overview

This exercise refers to the disability conditions covered by Exercises 1 to 8 in this section.

1 Which **one** of the conditions has an onset usually ranging from young adulthood to early middle age?

2 Name **three** of the conditions that are present from the moment of conception.

3 In which **two** of the conditions does the onset usually occur in late adulthood or old age?

4 Name **two** of the conditions that can lead to learning disabilities in childhood.

5 Name **two** of the conditions that could be prevented by genetic counselling.

Topic 3 Practitioners and provision

Exercise 1 Practioners

1 Which practitioner might help a child with cerebral palsy to speak more clearly?

2 How can a health visitor help to identify disability conditions in young children?

3 Which practitioner might advise an overweight client about suitable foods?

4 Which practitioner might assess the needs and eligibility of a client who might benefit from residential care?

5 Which practitioner arranges special education provision within a school?

Exercise 2 Types of provision

The statements in Questions **1–8** describe certain types of provision. In each case, name the provision.

1 An arrangement to give an informal carer a break of a few days

2 Long-term accommodation with nursing care

3 A school attended only by pupils with severe disabilities

4 A scheme providing grants to help disabled people start work

5 A cash benefit for disabled adults of working age to help pay for care and transport

6 Care and activities provided part-time outside the person's own home

7 Domestic and personal care provided part-time within the person's own home

8 A means-tested benefit for disabled people in work

Topic 4 Barriers, aids and adaptations

Exercise 1 Barriers, aids and adaptations

1 Suggest **two** adaptations, common in public buildings, which are designed to facilitate entry to the building for people in wheelchairs.

2 Suggest **two** learning resources that are difficult for partially sighted schoolchildren to use.

3 What is the name given to aids designed to help partially sighted people read printed text?

4 What is the purpose of audio description in cinemas?

5 Which aid must be used to receive information from a hearing induction loop system?

6 Give **two** aids designed to help maintain an upright posture when walking.

7 Suggest **one** way that a kitchen could be adapted for a person who uses a wheelchair.

8 Suggest **one** aid that a person with severe osteoarthritis could use to make it easier to get dressed and undressed.

Topic 5 Legislation

Exercise 1 The Disability Discrimination Act 1995

1 Which of the following form part of the provision of the Disability Discrimination Act (DDA)? Tick any that apply.
   a equal access to goods and services
   b the requirement to employ a quota of disabled people
   c equal rights to buy or rent property
   d equal opportunities for training at work

2 A small business has offices on the ground floor and the first floor of a building. The toilets are up the stairs on the first floor. Suggest a reasonable adjustment the employer might make for a new employee who uses a wheelchair and works in the ground-floor office.

3 On what grounds would an employer be justified in claiming that such an adjustment was not 'reasonable'?

4 Which legal body is set up to rule on cases of discrimination at work?

Exercise 2 The NHS and Community Care Act 1990

1 a The NHS and Community Care Act led to a change from care in institutions towards care in the…

b Under this Act, which bodies became the main purchasers of care services?

c Name the system set up under the Act to plan, provide and check care services.

d Give **three** criteria a social worker is likely to use when carrying out a needs assessment.

e Following a needs assessment, what is the next step, in which a practitioner finds out if a client is eligible for care?

2 Statements **a–c** describe stages involved in the provision and checking of care; in each case, name the stage.
a Checking that care is being provided as planned

b Providing the care

c Deciding if the provision has met the needs of the client and whether care should continue or be modified

In some examination papers, you are asked to draw conclusions from numerical data that are presented in a table.

Example question:
A survey of 100 individuals in each of three age groups was carried out that investigated four different kinds of treatment for eye disorders.

Age group (years)	Contact lenses	Single-focal glasses	Bifocal or varifocal glasses	Cataract surgery
20–39	21	27	0	0
40–59	20	37	14	2
60–79	6	18	43	16

Analyse the data in the table and draw conclusions about treatments for eye disorders in relation to age. *(6 marks)*

Data analysis

In this type of question, marks are not awarded for simply repeating the data in the table. For example, if you make the point that 21 of the 20–39-year-olds wore contact lenses, you will not receive any credit. Rather, you are required to make comparisons. In this case, the question asks you to make comparisons by age.

Although the question will not give you any more guidance on this, it is useful to think about the ways you could analyse the data by dividing them up into simple comparisons, proportional comparisons, indications of similarities, greatest and least scores, and the identification of trends.

Making simple 'more or less' comparisons

For example, you could say that far fewer 60–79-year-olds wore contact lenses than the younger age groups.

Overall comparisons are also useful. For example, you could point out that people in the 60–79-year-old age group received the most treatments overall.

Making proportional comparisons

You could be more specific and state that the number of people receiving one of these treatments in one age group is about half that (say), or twice that, in another group. For example, you could say that the use of contact lenses among 40–59-year-olds was at least three times greater than it was among 60–79-year-olds.

Indicating similarities

Note that comparisons can also be made when there are very small differences. Look at contact lens use among 20–39-year-olds compared with that among 40–59-year-olds. Here the difference is so small that it would be misleading to say that contact lens use was greater in the 20–39-year-olds. However, it would be worth pointing out that contact lens use in these two groups was 'very similar' or 'almost the same' or 'not very different'.

Indicating greatest or least

Marks are also likely to be available for pointing out the greatest or smallest figures. For example, you could point out that the 40–59-year-olds showed the greatest use of single-focal glasses.

Identifying trends

When age categories are given, it is sometimes possible to identify trends. For example, you could say that in the sample surveyed the use of bifocal or varifocal glasses increased with age.

There are more than six points that could be made about the data in the table but only 6 marks available. To increase your chances of receiving full marks, it is a good idea to make more than six points.

Exercise 1

To answer the questions in this exercise you should refer to the table of data at the beginning of this section.

1 Make **two** simple comparisons between the age groups in respect of using single-focal glasses.

2 Make **two** 'greatest or least' statements about the use of single-focal glasses.

3 Make **one** proportional comparison between the 40–59-year-olds and the 60–79-year-olds with respect to using single-focal glasses.

4 Make **one** proportional comparison with respect to cataract operations.

5 Indicate **one** trend in cataract operations.

Applying knowledge to data questions

As well as data analysis, you could be asked in a follow-up question to use knowledge when drawing conclusions. For example, you might be asked to explain some of the differences shown in the table. The data in the table on p. 49 show that bifocal or varifocal glasses were needed more by older people than by younger people. You could explain that this is because as people grow older, their eyes become less able to accommodate — a condition known as presbyopia.

Understanding tables

You should read the information given in data tables carefully; otherwise you might make mistaken assumptions.

The next exercise is designed to get you thinking more carefully about tables of data.

Exercise 2

To answer the questions in this exercise you should refer to the table of data at the beginning of this section.

1 You were told that 100 individuals in the 20–39-year age group were surveyed, yet the total number of treatments listed for this group adds up to 48, not 100. Why is this?

2 It turns out that only 38 people in the 20–39-year age group received any of the listed treatments, yet the data showing that 21 used contact lenses and 27 used single-focal glasses are correct. Explain this.